IMAGES OF ENGLAND

Ledbury

Ledbury from the Air.

All the Ledbury landmarks are easily seen on this 1923 aerial photograph of the town. The police station in Worcester Road has yet to built and there are very few houses along Bank Crescent below Dog Wood. (Pub. Airco Aerials Ltd, London)

IMAGES OF ENGLAND

Ledbury

Tim Ward

NONSUCH

First published 1996
This new pocket edition 2005
Images unchanged from first edition

Nonsuch Publishing Limited
The Mill, Brimscombe Port,
Stroud, Gloucestershire, GL5 2QG
www.nonsuch-publishing.com

British Library Cataloguing in Publication Data.
A catalogue record for this book is available from the British Library.

ISBN 1-84588-155-9

Typesetting and origination by Nonsuch Publishing Limited
Printed in Great Britain by Oaklands Book Services Limited

Contents

Introduction   7

1.   Ledbury   9
2.   Ledbury People and Events   39
3.   Churches and Chapels   51
4.   Royalty in Ledbury   59
5.   Leisure Activities   63
6.   Work   73
7.   The Railway   85
8.   World War One   89
9.   Surrounding Villages   95
10.   Stoke Edith   101
11.   Eastnor   105
12.   Bosbury   109
13.   Colwall   115
14.   Much Marcle   121

Much Marcle and Yatton Flower Show and Sports Day has always been a popular event in the local calendar. There was an annual road race from the Ledbury Market House to the show ground five miles away. Here the runners in the 1909 race line up in the High Street awaiting the start. (Pub. J. Tilley)

Acknowledgements

I am very grateful for the loan of postcards and photographs from Alan Hamblin, Olive Wiles, Roger Broomfield and Lens of Sutton, and for help and information from lots of friends and local people. Also I am eternally grateful to my wife, Shirley, for all the cups of coffee which fuelled this project.

Introduction

For the past one hundred years the charming little town of Ledbury has seen the production of thousands of postcards. I have collected photographic postcards of Ledbury and the surrounding area for many years and have selected some as the basis of this little book of Ledbury life during the first half of the twentieth century. I am not a historian so I apologise for any inadvertent mistakes.

Picture postcards were introduced in Great Britain in 1894. The first ones were small (115 x 89mm) with the stamp and address on one side and the message on the other. After 1902, when the Post Office regulations were relaxed, one side was reserved for the picture and the other for the address and message. The size was increased to 140 x 90mm.

Publishers were able to use this format much more effectively and a host of all sorts of postcards on every conceivable subject were issued.

Soon postcard collecting became a major hobby and King Edward's reign saw the golden age of the postcard. Most families seem to have possessed an album for their collection. Magazines catered for the craze much as they do today. Many beautiful cards were printed in Germany. Publishers produced cards on all sorts of themes: actresses, military, greetings, royalty, political, street scenes, views, flowers, trees, comics, glamour, novelty, hold to light, Father Christmas, mechanical, railways, etc. World War One saw an increase in political and patriotic cards and the beautiful embroidered silks made in France.

Picture postcards served several functions. A cheap and efficient postal service delivered mail the next day or locally on the same day it was posted. In the days when telephones were not available 'Meet me at 7 tonight' was not an uncommon message on an Edwardian postcard. Businessmen used them for advertising. Comic cards provided a means of sending risqué or personal messages to friends or relations. The increased availability of cameras meant local photographers could provide a unique record of local events when newspapers did not print photographs. Fortunately for later generations this also coincided with a period of considerable social and economic change.

A new generation after the war lost interest in postcards for a variety of reasons such as the increase in postage rates, the advent of the telephone and also their decline in quality. Whatever the reason, postcard collecting was neglected until twenty-five years ago when the Victoria and Albert museum staged an exhibition of postcards and the modern era of postcard collecting began.

As well as his studio portrait work, John Tilley photographed every local event possible during the first twenty years of the century. Obviously an astute businessman, he had a sharp eye for sales to local people. Most of his cards of events contained a number of people and were published within twenty-four hours so local sales were assured. Townspeople could write 'Can you see me on the picture?' and send them to friends and relations away from home to keep them up to date with the news. Postage was ½d. Printed postcards were ½d also, but the real photographic cards were usually 2d. Tilley's certainly were 2d. This initial price difference must account for their current scarcity. These are the cards that often provide the only record of events and scenes long gone and are recognised as valuable historical documents by museums and record offices. I do not think John Tilley or any of his contemporary photographers deliberately set out to record events and scenes for posterity. His personal collection would surely have contained much more than family photographs if he had intended this. We are indeed very fortunate that, by chance, his camera recorded so much information about his contemporary life in and around Ledbury. We owe all those early photographers an enormous debt of gratitude for the wealth of photographs of the early part of the twentieth century, when the country was changing from the time of the horse to the modern industrial age, without which most of the recent local history books could not have written.

Now that I no longer live in Ledbury I feel more than a little nostalgic and look forward to a chance to return. Of course it has changed as the century progressed but it still retains much of the small market town portrayed on the old cards.

Will Robinson poses with a fine display of meat outside his shop at 82 The Homend in 1920. Hygiene laws now thankfully prevent such health risks.

One

Ledbury

The Southend, c. 1908 when a girl and pram could safely stand in the street for the photographer, John Tilley, to take their picture. How the advent of the motor car has changed the tranquillity of our roads. (Pub. J. Tilley)

The Royal Oak Hotel in the Southend had its own petrol pumps in the yard supplying BP petrol for guests' cars. Note the magnificent lamp above the entrance. John Currie was landlord here in the 1920s.

A 1908 view of the Cross with a herd of shorthorn cattle being driven up the Worcester Road from the Market. (Pub. J. Tilley)

Herefordshire was traditionally a popular area for gypsies, partly because there was plenty of seasonal work on the farms. Here two gypsy caravans pause in the Southend, *c.* 1910. (Anon.)

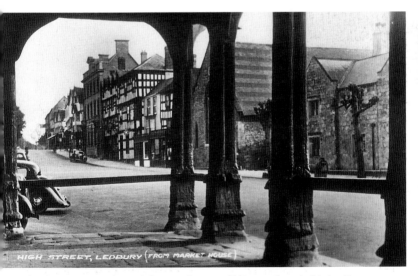

Only a few cars occupy the High Street in this quite 1940 scene from the Market House.

A Victorian photo (c. 1890) of the Top Cross and Hampton's boot and shoe shop. This was before the plaster was removed to reveal the attractive timbers beneath. Note the solid wheels on the handcart.

The Park, home of Lord Biddulph, on a 1908 postcard advertising the Royal Automobile Club's second provincial meeting there on Saturday 2 July. (Pub. J. Tilley)

76. The Worcester Road, Ledbury.

Worcester Road, 1912. A flock of sheep on their way to market pause for John Tilley to record the scene. Masefield's offices are still there, but the further houses have gone to accommodate the police station entrance and houses occupy the orchard on the right. (Pub. J. Tilley)

New Street, *c.* 1935. The Steppes timbers are now fully revealed. The Old Talbot has become the Talbot, and Charles Lee was the popular landlord of the Vine Tap, now a Chinese takeaway.

The Steppes, New Street in 1909, when A.R. Green lived there. He was Medical Officer for the area. (Pub. J. Tilley)

A herd of cattle approach the market down New Street in 1908. Ledbury Mineral Water Company occupied the buildings on the left of the street. (Pub. J. Tilley)

A 1923 view of the Market House. It was built in 1633 of local oak and it still houses a busy weekly market. (Pub. Doncaster Rotophoto Co.)

The Talbot Inn in New Street. The Post Office was in New Street, next to the parked car, until 1930. Later this was the Midland Electricity Board showroom and is now a thriving newsagents.

Mrs Barbara Hamblin ran this little sweet shop at 22 New Street about 1900. Subsequently her husband Thomas Charles owned a bootmakers business here for several years. In the doorway stands Lillian Hamblin aged six, her brother aged eight and Archibold who was killed in the First World War.

Above: Hopkins & Sons Carriage and
Motor Works in New Street in 1908, with
workmen, cars and carriages lined up
outside. Only the brick building on the left
remains. A superstore was built on the site in
1988. (Pub. J. Tilley)

Right: Church Lane in 1904. This charming
scene has scarcely altered in ninety years,
although the fashions certainly have!

Church Lane, Ledbury   Valentines Series

*I can't write to-night as I said. I haven't
been out since Sunday so I have to go*

THE WHITE STREAK SHEWS THE PASSAGE OF A BICYCLE LAMP.

HIGH STREET, LEDBURY. PHOTOGRAPH TAKEN AT 10·30 AT NIGHT. JULY 1st 1908.

Ledbury High Street, 10.30 p.m., 1 July 1908. Controversy still surrounds the origin of the extraordinary light effects which permitted John Tilley to take a series of photographs of the High Street. Was it an explosion of a meteorite or a UFO over Northern Russia or a very bright Aurora Borealis? Shall we ever know? The phenomena was visible across Northern Europe. (Pub. J. Tilley)

THE WHITE STREAK SHEWS THE PASSAGE OF A BICYCLE LAMP.

1175. HIGH STREET, LEDBURY. PHOTOGRAPH TAKEN AT 11 AT NIGHT. JULY 1st 1908.

POST CARD

CORRESPONDENCE

ADDRESS ONLY

A Miracle of Photography.—Aurora Borealis Pictures.

Photographs taken at 10.30 & 11 p.m.

"The Sketch," July 22, 1908, under the above heading, gives reproductions of the Photo on the other side and a companion Picture, with the following descriptive remarks :—

"These extraordinary photographs were taken during the display of Aurora Borealis on July 1. The phenomenon is one of the most mysterious in nature, and scientists are still divided as to its cause. On July 1 the whole of the northern sky was lit up until long past midnight by a brilliant white glow, which made it possible to read even after 11 p.m. The phenomenon was observed all over northern and central Europe, and it was accompanied by a surprising depression of the barometer. The white streak in the photographs marks the course of a bicycle lamp.—

Tilley & Son, Photo., Ledbury."

Mr Smith
The Pool Farm
Acton Beauchamp
Nr Worcester

A busy market-day scene in the High Street in 1906. Two years later the plaster was removed from The Feathers, revealing the traditional view we know today. (Pub. J. Tilley)

A 1920s view down the High Street as the motor car starts to intrude on the scene. (Pub. Raphael Tuck & Sons, London)

Ledbury, Market House & Barrett Browning Institute

Above: A busy market-day scene beside the Market House in Edwardian times. This same flock of sheep appears superimposed on the other street scenes published by J. Tilley.

Right: As a memorial to Elizabeth Barratt-Browning, the Institute, which now houses the library, was erected by public subscription in 1890. It cost just over £3,000 to build. This is a 1907 view. (Pub. J. Tilley)

Above: An ice-cream salesman finds trade slow outside the Market House in the summer of 1939.

Left: This black-and-white timbered shop at the bottom of Church Lane opposite the Market House was demolished around 1890. It belonged to William Smith, hairdresser and fancy goods salesman.

Opposite above: Motor cars and coaches line up along the High Street and the Homend as horse power gives way to the internal combustion engine, *c.* 1930.

Opposite below: Two Victorian children give their donkey a well-earned rest at the water trough outside St Catherine's almshouses. The railings were removed for scrap metal in World War Two. The water pump on the pavement has also disappeared. The donkey cart was made of wickerwork for lightness.

A child checks her boot for something nasty as she crosses a quiet Bye Street, a very different scene now since the motor car has taken over. Most of the buildings have gone too, giving a changed atmosphere to this calm scene.

This row of cottages stood opposite the cattle market in Bye Street across the entrance to the modern Masefield Close. (Pub. J. Tilley)

Above: The Brewery Inn is little changed since this 1910 photograph, but the cottages beyond are now the site of the fire station.

Right: The old gives way to the new as an Austin delivery van overtakes a bullock cart in the Homend, *c.* 1935. Note the width of the Herefords' horns.

The Daw Brothers ran a carpentry and joinery business in Market Street for many years.
(Pub. J. Tilley)

The Ledbury Girl Guides parade in front of the *Ledbury Reporter* offices in the Homend,
awaiting the arrival of Queen Mary after her stay at Eastnor Castle, in July 1937.

These terrace houses in Bye Street have hardly changed since this 1910 photograph. Note the shutters on the ground floor windows. (Pub. J. Tilley)

As part of his local empire John Tilley ran an advertising service posting bills on walls and hoardings. This 'Posting Station' was in Bye Street. (Pub. J. Tilley)

An unusual photograph of the building of Brynderwyn in Woodleigh Road in 1926–27.
Mr Staunton, the builder, erected this house at a cost of £600. (Anon.)

Woodleigh Road in the winter snow.

Another busy view of the High Street on a market day in 1930. St Katherine's almshouses on the left were built in 1822 to replace earlier buildings.

A flock of sheep being driven along the Homend was a regular sight on market days until the arrival of livestock lorries in the 1930s. (Pub. J. Tilley)

Crowds flock to Ledbury Fair every year. In 1912 they were amused by the films at J. Jones' bioscope show.

The Homend in the 1920s when deliveries were made by horse and cart. Shop names have changed in the past seventy years but the buildings remain virtually the same. (Pub. Smith, The Homend)

Increasing numbers of motor cars necessitated new Belisha beacons in the Homend to help pedestrians cross Ledbury's now-busy street, July 1936.

Austin Maddox outside his seed shop at 8 The Homend, *c.* 1910. His seeds certainly gave excellent results judging by the display. This shop was demolished in the 1930s to make room for Woolworths.

Conroy Williams used this view of his comfortable, well-furnished dining room as an advertising card to encourage patronage of the Plough Hotel on Tuesday market days. (Pub. J. Tilley)

The much-loved Cottage Hospital photographed in 1923 shows little external change. This was built by Lord Biddulph in 1892 to commemorate his son's coming of age. (Pub. J. Tilley)

A roadmaking gang in the Homend near the Plough, c. 1925.

A similar photograph of the Homend in 1924. Harris' shop has now closed. (Pub. Doncaster Rotophoto Co.)

The Boys School in the Homend was built in 1867 and enlarged in 1894. George Paul was headmaster and lived in the schoolhouse when this photograph was taken in 1909. Retirement flats now occupy the site. (Pub. J. Tilley)

A group of farm animals on the way to market outside William Harris' shop at 114 The Homend in 1910.

The Lower Cross on a busy market day, c. 1906. A small herd of calves are on their way from market to a local farm, and a variety of farm carts are parked in the streets. (Pub. J. Tilley)

Frank Swift sold and repaired bicycles, cars, farm machinery and general ironmongery for many years at his garage in the Homend.

A mechanic changes a van's rear wheel while the lady driver waits outside Weston's garage, c. 1920. It has hardly changed in appearance since it was built, but it is unlikely it can still supply 'Any make of car, motor cycle and all replacement parts' as the advertisement announces.

David Smith was Ledbury's largest building contractor and also owned a saw-mill in the Homend. Here he poses with some of his premises, now the site of Spicers.

The Knapp, the birthplace of John Masefield, still has the air of tranquillity shown on this 1910 photo by J. Tilley.

The bottom of Belle Orchard, *c.* 1920.

These attractive seventeenth-century cottages in Church Street were replaced in 1974 by modern complex of old peoples' flats. Just visible beyond in this Edwardian photograph are the gable ends of the Girls School, which was demolished in 1983 to be replaced by modern houses.

Two

Ledbury People and Events

A total of 168 girls pose for their annual photograph in 1912, watched by the headmistress, Miss Hooper. (Pub. J. Tilley)

Alan Hamblin enjoys his second birthday present in the garden of his home in Brynderwyn, Woodleigh Road, 1937.

Studio photograph of two little girls and their favourite toys. (Pub. J. Tilley)

A children's garden party at Oaklands, William Tilley's home in the Homend. The children copy their elders in a game of soldiers in camp with their mothers acting as nurse and cook. Even the dog guards a tent. Teddy in the car is about to take the salute!

The real thing! The Ledbury company of the Herefordshire Regiment enjoy their annual camp at Patcham in Sussex, c. 1910. (Pub. Brighton View Co.)

The Ledbury Boys Scouts parade beside the Market House, *c.* 1912. Note the ladders hanging on the far posts for fire-fighting and rescue.

Geology students examine the limestone strata in the quarry beside the Malvern Road during a field study camp in March 1932.

The RAC's second provincial meeting attracted about fifty cars on 11 July 1908. They were lined up in the Southend while their drivers visited the Park garden at Lord Biddulph's invitation. (Pub. J. Tilley)

ARRIVAL
OF
THE MAIL
COACH.
1790

A carnival scene in the Park in the 1920s, depicting the arrival of the first mail coach in the town in 1790.

VOTE FOR CLIVE
AND SPEED THE PLOUGH.

Polling in the 1910 General Election was on a cold January day. Captain Clive's supporters have a free if uncomfortable ride to the polls. The Liberals won 274 seats, the Conservatives 273, Irish Nationalists 82 and the Labour Party 41 seats. (Pub. J. Tilley)

Opposite above: A sit down meal in the Homend, *c.* 1900 for an unknown celebration. Such a meal would be quite impossible because of today's motor traffic.

Opposite below: The January 1910 election aroused passion across the country as the issues of Irish Home Rule, votes for women and Free Trade were debated. This was reflected in postcards published locally and nationally. Captain Clive, the Conservative candidate, canvassed for votes at meetings in local halls and events such as the Trumpet Ploughing Match. He supported local farmers and hop growers against foreign competition. (Pub. J. Tilley)

Captain Clive won the seat with a majority of 395. Here is his triumphal arrival in Ledbury after the result was published. Evidently the authorities were expecting crowd trouble. On a card from R. Paul, the school master, to his sister he writes, 'This little town is packed and we have a force of about 25 extra police, quite a lot for us!' (Pub. J. Tilley)

The procession in the High Street during the dedication of Ledbury's new ambulance, June 1936.

I wonder if such a crowd would turn up these days to hear an election result? Most of the towns people seem to be outside the Market House for the 1910 election. (Pub. J. Tilley)

More decorations along New Street for the procession of local dignitaries and businessmen to the show. (Pub. J. Tilley)

Before the National Health Service was established in 1948 hospitals depended on direct public support. All sorts of collections, fêtes and processions were held to provide funds. The local Territorial Army held a church parade on 18 July to raise funds watched by townspeople in their Sunday best. (Pub. J. Tilley)

Street decorations at the Top Cross in June 1911 for the Herefordshire and Worcestershire Show held that year for three days at Hazle farm, Ledbury. (Pub. J. Tilley)

An impressive line-up of Hereford bulls awaits the judges eye. Note the horns. The modern breed is now polled. (Pub. J. Tilley)

A shire horse awaits his entry to the judging ring at the show. (Pub. J. Tilley)

Choirs from a dozen nearby parishes process out of Ledbury Church after the Herefordshire Choral Union's triannual festivals in June 1908. A crowd of friends and townspeople watch with interest. (Pub. J. Tilley)

Three

Churches and Chapels

Beautiful floral decorations in St Michael's church for the 1907 Harvest Festival. (Pub. J. Tilley)

"O.P."-60510 OLD VICARAGE. LEDBURY

Above: The Old Vicarage,
Ledbury. (Pub. Doncaster Rotophoto Co.)

Left: The Revd Frederick Carnegy MA, rector of
St Michael's and rural dean. (Pub. J. Tilley)

Opposite above: St Michael's church choir in
1908 pose outside the Norman west door on the
church. (Pub. J. Tilley)

Opposite below: Some of the choirs attending
Ledbury's choral festivities in procession to the
church in 1908. (Pub. J. Tilley)

LEDBURY CHURCH CHOIR 1908.

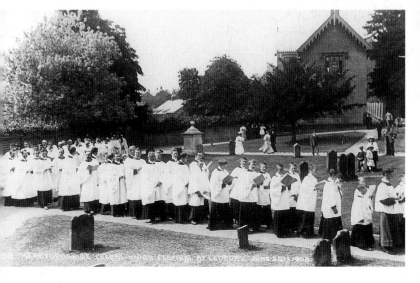

HEREFORDSHIRE FRIENDLY UNION FESTIVAL AT LEDBURY. JUNE 25th 1908.

Ledbury church Fancy Fair was held in the Park on July 15 1909 to raise money for the Church Room which was built and opened the following year. These ladies await customers at their sweet stall. (Pub. J. Tilley)

The Church Lads Brigade man their rifle range at the 1909 Fancy Fair to help raise funds. (Pub. J. Tilley)

Another fund-raising event for the church was a very good production of the *Pied Piper* in the Royal Hall, November 1909. Here fifty-three of the cast pose for publicity photographs. (Pub. J. Tilley)

Ledbury Church Fancy Fair was held in St Katherine's Hall, 23–24 April 1908. This shows Mrs L. Tilley's fancy work stall. (Pub. J. Tilley)

The Ledbury Church Lads Brigade, *c.* 1908.

St Michael's church, set on a hill overlooking the town.

Right: The Wesleyan chapel in the Homend in 1904. (Pub. J. Tilley)

Below: The interior of the Baptist Chapel in 1904. (Pub. J. Tilley)

Ledbury Wesleyans presented an 'Olde English Fayre' in June 1936, when Revd George Sherwell was in charge of the church.

Unusual interior view of the Mission Hall in Bye Street in 1915. The Message reads, 'Built many years ago by Lady Henry Somerset for undenomination work. She gave it up about 12 years ago and we have carried it on ever since.' (Pub. J. Tilley)

Four

Royalty in Ledbury

Crowds in their best clothes mass by the Market House for the coronation festivities of King George V, June 22 1911. (Pub. J. Tilley)

Left: The crowds celebrating King George V's Silver Jubilee in the Homend 1935.

Below: Dorothy Hamblin, Arthur Hamblin, Mrs Hamblin and son Alan aged six weeks, Sarah Baker, and Margaret Hamblin aged three, await the Silver Jubilee procession outside the Almshouses, July 1935.

Enthusiastic crowds at the railway station entrance as the royal party returns to their train.

Queen Mary's Rolls Royce driving up the Homend.

The visit of the Duke and Duchess of York to Ledbury in June 1934. Three years later they were crowned King George VI and Queen Elizabeth after his brother's abdication.

The local police were on crowd-control duty as Queen Mary drove up the Homend after her visit to Eastnor Castle, July 1937.

Five

Leisure Activities

The Ledbury Hunt Puppy Show in 1910, when Sir George Bullough, Captain Warren and Thomas Peacock were joint masters. (Pub. J. Tilley)

Ledbury Hunt Open Day at the kennels, 1909. The back of the station with the white-washed cattle pens can just be seen behind the kennels. Fifty three and a half couples (107 dogs) was a very large pack to hunt. (Pub. J. Tilley)

Ledbury Hunt Puppy Show at the kennels sited behind the station on the Bromyard road, 11 July 1910. (Pub. J. Tilley)

Meet of Mr Gordon Cumming's private pack of hounds at Ledbury railway station, 1 May 1909. (Pub. J. Tilley)

They start them young in Ledbury! This child's toy horse is no taller than the hounds he wants to hunt with at the opening meet of the Ledbury Hounds at the Down House, 8 November 1909. (Pub. J. Tilley)

Boxing Day meet of the Ledbury Hounds at the Feathers Hotel in 1910, a popular colourful event. (Pub. J. Tilley)

Ledbury Hunt Races in 1908 drew the usual enthusiastic crowd of spectators for the local farmers races. (Pub. J. Tilley)

Mr Arthur Thomas Hamblin, seated second from the right, was a telegraphist at the GPO for many years. One of his interests was running this orchestra, which played at dances in the town between 1920-26.

Ledbury Choral Society in 1931.

Ledbury Junior football team pose at their Jubilee Meadow ground beside the Gloucester railway line for a team photograph, 1907.

Ledbury Town Football Club, 1910.

Ledbury Town Football Club, c. 1920.

After a comic Ladies vs Gentlemen charity football match in 1936, Mr Arthur Hamblin introduces the participants to Mrs Masefield for their prizes.

Above: W.O. Richardson, a star player for West Bromwich Albion, referees the annual charity match between the Post Office and the Railway. His wife kicks off at Ledbury Town ground on 12 May 1937. These annual matches were organised by Arthur Hamblin to raise funds for the local hospital for several years in the 1930s.

Left: Young and old all gather round the flagstaff by the Market House for patriotic Empire Day speeches in 1916. (Pub. J. Tilley)

Ledbury Town Cricket Club, c. 1921. (Pub. J. Tilley)

Half-way up the hill a section of the large crowd watches Cecil Edge's efforts to be the fastest up. These postcards were on sale the following day at 2d each. (Pub. J. Tilley)

These two Daimler cars were the fastest in the Herefordshire Automobile Club's hill climb at Fromes Hill on Friday 3 May 1907. (Pub. Daimler Motor Co.)

This event was very well attended as the crowded scene at the bottom of the hill shows. (Pub. J. Tilley)

Six

Work

As the brewing industry grew, so hop-growers developed from small scale acreage on most farms to large-scale operations in suitable areas of the country, mostly in Kent, Sussex and Herefordshire. Large numbers of people were needed for short periods to pick the hops. To pick the local hops people came from the towns of South Wales, the Black Country and Birmingham to join gypsies and local people. Here farm carts transport hop pickers from Ledbury station to farms at Bosbury. (Pub. J. Tilley)

Like much of British agriculture, hop growing has changed considerably since 1900. Originally hops were grown up long poles. Now they grow up strings attached to overhead wires and all the harvesting is performed by machinery. (Pub. J. Tilley)

Hop picking used to be a very social affair, as well as providing extra income for local families. This is the Hamblin family hop-picking in 1936.

All the family worked together in the hopyards as even children as young as five or six could earn a few pennies for the family budget. (Pub. J. Tilley)

In contrast to the previous photo, better-off families could treat a day's hopping almost as a picnic. Large floral hats, ties and spotless white blouses were the order of the day. (Pub. J. Tilley)

The Ledbury area is well suited to fruit growing and has produced fruit for the Midlands and South Wales markets for many years. Here a large number of women and children strawberry-pickers pose for the photographer. (Pub. J. Tilley)

'Dinner time' for a well-dressed group of local lady strawberry pickers in 1907. The fruit was destined for Hartley's Jam factory in Aintree. (Pub. J. Tilley)

A tree-felling gang from Clun led by Reg Breece and Alf Corfield pose beside a tree they were felling with their 7½ lb axes in Ledbury Park in 1905.

Before the market opened in 1887 cattle and sheep were sold in the street beside the Market House. The cattle market was an important centre for local farmers. Lomas & Anthony were the auctioneers in this 1904 photo, to be succeded by Pope Smith & Anthony, and later C.T. Smith. A housing complex has since been built here. (Pub. J. Tilley)

Ledbury Post Office staff pictured outside St Catherine's Almshouses in the High Street in 1910. Mr Bell the postmaster wears the light suit in the centre of the picture. On his right is Mr E.J. Smith, overseer and postmaster from 1920. The big man on the right was George Hill, who did the Berrow, Hollybush and Eastnor round. The motor vehicles were leased from Will Tilley, the photographer's brother. Also in the picture are Charles Jones, Fred Watson, Mr Hankin, Harry Jessett, Teddy Smith, Bob Hewkett, Reg Summers, W. Jessett and son Charles, Bill Lewis, Harry Davies, Frank Reeves, Fred Jessett, Will Smith, Albert Chad, George Watkins and Ernest Hill. (Pub. J. Tilley)

Chauffeur and grooms pose with their master's magnificent landaulette near Ledbury. (Pub. J. Tilley)

Hay was the fuel for transport during the days of real horse power. A Barford's hay press is in use here on a local farm trussing hay for South Wales pit ponies. The man on the left cut a section of hay from the stack with the hay knife. Placed in the press, it was compressed by the ratchet handle on the right and the strings tied by hand. It was a long slow laborious winter job now performed in the field at haytime by machinery.

Above: 'This is the Butler, Valet and Footman here. The Butler was 82 on Sat,' reads the message on the back of this card posted 25 February 1908. But who are they and where did they work? (Pub. J. Tilley)

Right: Work in the large houses was one of the few opportunities available to girls. Going into service at £20–£25 per year at least meant they had a regular job. These smart young maids look happy enough as they pose for their photo, *c.* 1908. (Pub. J. Tilley)

F.C. Flower farmed at New Mills and was also a haulage contractor. Here his Fowler traction engine pauses on its way to Mitcheldean with a huge piece of machinery for the cement works there. Posted 15 December 1906.

Opposite above: John Tilley's advertising staff pose besides on the his hoardings at the bottom of the station approach, a very eye-catching site for rail travellers. Among other things he carried on a lucrative business as an advertising contractor. (Pub. J. Tilley)

Opposite below: A farmworker stops with his team at the end of a day's work drilling peas.

William Tilley poses with his new Darracq hire car in 1908. His garage was in the corner of the cattle market. It is now a saleroom. (Pub. J. Tilley)

An eight-ton coal wagon built in 1897 by Gloucester Railway Carriage and Wagon Co. for James Griffin who ran a coal business at the station yard, Ledbury.

Seven

The Railway

J.B. Sherlock photograph of Ledbury Station in 1919, showing the building and track layout in its heyday.

Ledbury Town Halt in Bye Street on the Gloucester branch line was built on top of the Hereford and Gloucester canal. This site is now covered by a landscape garden. Beyond the bridge is a public walk. (Pub. Lens of Sutton)

A view of the north end of the Ledbury Tunnel, where the accident described on the next page occurred. (Pub. Sherlock)

Above: This spectacular accident is described by railway enthusiasts as a deliberate derailment. The brakes on a goods train to Swansea failed as it approached Ledbury Tunnel. To prevent a serious accident inside the tunnel the signalman diverted the train onto a safety siding above the track, where it overturned. Only minor injuries resulted to the crew but the noise is said to have woken all Ledbury. (Pub. J. Tilley)

Right: Great Western Railway luggage labels, c. 1900.

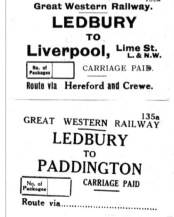

135a

Great Western Railway.

LEDBURY

TO

Liverpool, Lime St. L. & N.W.

No. of Packages   CARRIAGE PAID.

Route via Hereford and Crewe.

135a

GREAT WESTERN RAILWAY

LEDBURY

TO

PADDINGTON

No. of Packages   CARRIAGE PAID

Route via ....

RAILWAY ACCIDENT AT LEDBURY. MAY 10TH 08.

A goods-train accident occurred at the west end of the viaduct on 10 May 1908. A wagon coupling broke on the descent to Ledbury Tunnel from Colwall. Seeing something was wrong, the Ledbury signalman halted the front part of the train at Rea bridge beyond the viaduct. The runaway rear part of the train gathered speed through the station and a violent collision with the stationary part was inevitable. Fortunately no one was hurt but it took some time to recover the wagons and repair the track. (Pub. J. Tilley)

G. W. R.	G. W. R.	G.W.R.
Stoke Edith	**Ashperton**	**Colwall**

Great Western Railway luggage labels, c. 1910.

Eight

World War One

Sixteen National reservists parade outside the TA in New Street three months after the start of World War One. A small group of well wishers look on without much fervour. (Pub. J. Tilley)

Above: Their kitbags piled on a cart, the Ledbury Territorials muster outside the TA headquarters in New Street two days after the outbreak of World War One. Families and friends wish them good luck and watch as they make ready to depart. (Pub. J. Tilley)

Below: The Westminster Boy Scouts Band cheerfully play as the territorials march to the railway station along the flag-decorated High Street. Most of the townspeople turned out to watch. Patriotic fervour ran high and 'their boys' were expected home by Christmas. (Pub. J. Tilley)

The troops await the train to take them to the war as the station platform fills with their families. (Pub. J. Tilley)

A convoy of at least fifteen army lorries parked in the High Street in 1915 was watched by an interested crowd. Beneath the 'Garage' sign Tilley's advertise '20 open or closed cars for hire', 'Postcards' and 'Goss crested china'. (Pub. J. Tilley)

The Great War soon sucked huge numbers of soldiers into the conflict in France and Belgium. There was also considerable paranoia about German spies and saboteurs. It is easy therefore to understand the enthusiasm of the Ledbury Church Lads Brigade to go to the Elan Valley dams to guard Birmingham's water supply. The are seen here leaving Ledbury Station on 20 August 1914.

In 1915 and 1916 this donkey and cart was auctioned hundreds of times to raise money for the Red Cross in Ledbury and in the neighbouring towns. Belonging to M.R. Lane of Bosbury, it travelled as far afield as Crickhowell and Worcester raising funds. (Pub. J. Tilley)

The huge numbers of casualties in World War One created an acute shortage of hospital beds throughout Great Britain. Large houses everywhere were converted to military hospitals and convalescent homes. Lord Biddulph gave Upper Hall to be used in this way. Here a group of nurses and wounded soldiers pose outside Upper Hall in March 1915. (Pub. J. Tilley)

The well-known war memorial in the High Street to the seventy-one Ledbury servicemen who were killed. (Pub. J. Tilley)

LEDBURY EX-SERVICE MEN'S CHILDREN'S XMAS TREAT, 1921.

Dear *Dorothy Casamon*

We shall expect you at our Christmas Treat at 3.30 p.m., at the Royal Hall, on Thursday, December 29th.

Do come, it will be very nice.

No child admitted without Card.

An invitation to the 1921 Ex-Service Men's Children's Treat at the Royal Hall.

Nine

Surrounding Villages

Preston Court, c. 1920. The plaster has now been removed from the front to reveal the oak timbers beneath. (Pub. William Call, Monmouth)

Meet of the Ledbury Hounds at the Trumpet, 1909. (Pub. J. Tilley)

The Ledbury Hounds hunted a wide area of countryside around Ledbury. Here they meet at the Duke of York near Birtsmorton. (Pub. J. Tilley)

Farm yard scene at Stretton Court, c. 1915. (Pub. J. Tilley)

Firemen at Aylton farm fire.

Ledbury firemen rake over the still smouldering embers of a disastrous farm fire at Arthur Yapp's farm at Aylton, November 1906.

Elizabeth Barrett-Browning's father built this ornate house at Hope End in 1809 after buying the estate. Elizabeth spent her formative years in this beautiful locality. This was replaced by a larger house in 1873, which was completely destroyed by fire in April 1910. (Pub. J. Tilley)

Home Farm, Coddington, *c.* 1914.

Peaceful summer scene in Bromsberrow in 1910. (Pub. J. Tilley)

Exterior view of Donnington Hall, c. 1908. (Pub. J. Tilley)

Canon Frome Post Office served a village of 120 people. Standing in the doorway is Mrs Ellen Reeves the sub-postmistress. The donkey cart belongs to Mr G. Jones of Little Novering Farm. (Pub. J. Tilley)

Ashperton railway station in 1919 when William Hudson was station master. Now it is all dismantled and even the lines are reduced to a single track. (Pub. Sherlock)

Ten

Stoke Edith

The Hamlet, Stoke Edith. (Pub. Savory, Hereford)

Above: Another view of Stoke Edith Park. (Pub. J. Tilley)

Left: Queen Anne's bed, part of the luxurious interior of Stoke Edith Park. (Pub. J. Tilley)

Opposite above: Estate workers practiced every day with their old-fashioned manual fire-pump on Lady Foley's Stoke Edith estate. This proved to be of little use when the mansion caught fire early in the morning of 16 December 1927. A severe frost had frozen the pipes and hydrants, and the fire spread so rapidly before the Hereford and Ledbury appliances arrived that there was little they could do to prevent total destruction. (Pub. J. Tilley)

Opposite below: Stoke Edith Park, the home of the Foley family, faced these beautiful geometric gardens. A disastrous fire gutted the mansion in 1927 and it was never rebuilt. (Pub. J. Tilley)

STOKE EDITH PARK OLD FIRE ENGINE. NO. 2

Stoke Edith Park and Geometrical Gardens.

339 c

Railway workers pause during shunting operations in Stoke Edith sidings. Note the cattle trucks are whitewashed for hygiene reasons. (Anon.)

Eleven

Eastnor

These pretty timber-framed cottages in Eastnor are everyone's idea of a typical Herefordshire village. This was Wain Street in 1910. (Pub. J. Tilley)

599 LORD SOMERS COMING OF AGE FESTIVITIES, EASTNOR MAY 1908.

A delightful photograph of Lord Somer's family, friends and tenants outside Eastnor School taken during his coming of age festivities. (Pub. J. Tilley)

The whole population of 491 seems to have come to the coronation celebrations in Eastnor Park on 2 June 1911. The bowls club now use the pavilion. The green appears to be marked out for tennis. (Pub. J. Tilley)

The heavy clay in Eastnor Park can be a problem in wet weather. Here the Worcestershire Yeomanry dig themselves out of the mud stirred up by their horses during their 1912 annual camp. (Pub. J. Tilley)

The twenty-eight members of Eastnor church choir pose with the rector B.C. Hallowes in 1908. (Pub. J. Tilley)

Above: Boy Scout Jamboree, Whit Monday 1937. The Bishop of Hereford conducts divine service for the scouts in Eastnor Park.

Left: Lord Baden-Powell, the chief scout, and the Crown Prince of Rumania at the Jamboree in Eastnor Park, Whit Monday, 1937.

Twelve

Bosbury

Uriah Cosford sits in his delivery cart with his staff outside Bosbury village stores, where the villagers could purchase all their requirements, in 1909. A garage now stands on the site. (Pub. J. Tilley)

An action photograph of a Ladies *vs* Gentlemen's cricket match at Bosbury on 17 June 1909.
(Pub. J. Tilley)

Bosbury Ladies cricket team, *c.* 1920, dressed more comfortably in whites as attitudes and
fashions had changed.

Prize-winning shire mare and foal at Bosbury in 1907. (Pub. J. Tilley)

Opening meet of the North Ledbury Hounds at Bosbury House, 1910. (Pub. J. Tilley)

Miss Arrowsmith, the local schoolmistress on the right of the photo, staged a school production of Aladdin in 1909. The children here all look pretty serious about it in spite of their colourful costumes. (Pub. J. Tilley)

The first City of Westminster troop of boy scouts camped at Catley in July 1914. Their stay was interrupted by the outbreak of World War One. They returned home to London on 5 August where 'crowds of people were singing in the streets', according to the message. (Pub. J. Tilley)

Above: The local band heads the procession of Bosbury people to the church on 23 April 1916 to unveil a tablet to the local heroes. (Pub. J. Tilley)

Right: A disastrous fire broke out in Bosbury church on 12 July 1917. Prompt action by villagers saved many of the fittings and furniture before the Ledbury fire brigade quenched the flames. Five years elapsed before the church was fully restored. (Pub. J. Tilley)

Bosbury Church, partly destroyed by fire. July 12.1917

Above: Philip Clissett's crowded little workshop at Staplow. Crammed full of his tools and his partly-built chairs, this is where he carried on his craft for seventy years. He was born in Birtsmorton in 1817 and moved to Bosbury in 1838. Now his chairs are very sought after. (Pub. J. Tilley)

Left: Philip Clissett sits in his favourite chair by the pump in his garden. (Pub. J. Tilley)

Thirteen

Colwall

British Camp Hotel is still as popular for refreshments as in 1909. The message reads 'The photo is one of a series taken on a Whitsun cycling trip this year. It WAS hot.'

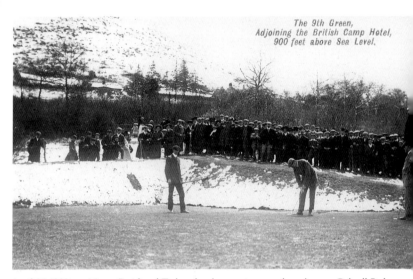

The 9th Green,
Adjoining the British Camp Hotel,
900 feet above Sea Level.

April 24 1908 saw Messrs Braid and Taylor play the opening round on the new Colwall Park golf course. Snow covered the Malverns but this was not enough to deter the enthusiastic crowd. This spectacular course disappeared during the depression of the 1920s. (Pub. J. Tilley)

The Royal Well Brewery at West Malvern, c. 1904. (Pub. J. Tilley)

Not everyone could squeeze into the church for the dedication ceremony, so many were forced to stand on the hill outside. (Pub. J. Tilley)

The dedication of the new church on 29 March 1910 saw a large procession headed by the local clergy walk from the village up the hill to the Wyche. Large crowds lined the road and all the local organizations took part. (Pub. J. Tilley)

Colwall Church Lads' Brigade, May 1910. (Pub. J. Tilley)

Colwall Station as seen by J.B. Sherlock on 15 July 1919. He was an enthusiastic railway photographer. Considerable changes have rendered it almost unrecognizable, as only the nearside platform and the footbridge remain. One track and all the buildings have gone. But Colwall can be deemed fortunate in having a railway station at all. Forty of the forty-four railway stations that once existed in Herefordshire have disappeared completely.

Because of the large number of wounded soldiers returning from the battles in France, large numbers of country houses were converted to Red Cross Hospitals to meet the need. Brand Lodge, the home of William d'Egville, was used as a temporary hospital until the end of the war. Most of the nurses were local girls, who pose here with thirty convalescent soldiers. (Pub. J. Tilley)

Lt. Col. J. Scott-Bowden, owner of the Park Hotel, must have thought a tremendous lot of his old horse to have this very unusual postcard published.

Colwall Park Hotel and Golf Club House, *c.* 1909, when Mrs W. Brown was manageress. (Pub. J. Tilley)

Everyone in their Sunday best enjoying the church fête at the Redlands, Colwall, July 1910. (Pub. J. Tilley)

Fourteen

Much Marcle

Much Marcle Football Club outside the Walwyn Arms, 1924–25.

Above: Much Marcle church. (Pub. William Call, Monmouth)

Left: The ancient cross. (Pub. William Call, Monmouth)

Carting hay at Lyne Down, Yatton in 1910.

The Great War Memorial Hall was built in 1921 at a cost of £2,300 as a tribute to all the local men who died in the war, and has since served the village well. (Anon.)

Runners line up beside the Market House to race to Much Marcle flower show.
(Pub. J. Tilley)

Crowds still throng to the Much Marcle and Yatton flower show in August as they did in this
busy 1910 scene. The sideshows are different but just as much fun. (Pub. J. Tilley)

Two Powell sisters pose in John Tilley's car outside Moor Court Farm in 1909. (Pub. J. Tilley)

12, MUCH MARCLE FLOWER SHOW. HORSE JUMPING.

Horse-jumping at the 1908 Much Marcle Flower Show. (Pub. J. Tilley)

George Toone, the landlord, stands in the doorway of the Walwyn Arms Hotel in 1926. (Anon.)

Much Marcle Post Office and Stores in 1926 when Mrs Florence Tarling was sub-postmistress. A quite rural scene as the postman prepares to cycle his round. (Anon.)

Weston's superbly dressed lorry visited Gloucester and Ross-on-Wye carnivals in 1925 and carried off the prizes, certainly putting 'Bounds Brand' cider on the map! (Anon.)

Much Marcle Cricket Club 1924. From right to left, top row: Frank Taylor, Ernie Cox, Percy Hawkins, Ed Brown, Harold Turner, Rupert Powell, Mr Tarling. Seated: Owen Jones, Harold Hawkins, Stafford Weston, Jack Taylor and Percy Wells.

Much Marcle Football Club pose with their 1920–21 season trophies outside the Walwyn Arms.